Dinosaurs Alive!
Velociraptor
and Other Speedy Killers

Jinny Johnson

Illustrated by Graham Rosewarne

Smart Apple Media

Smart Apple Media is published by Black Rabbit Books
P.O. Box 3263, Mankato, Minnesota 56002

Designed by Helen James
Edited by Mary-Jane Wilkins
Artwork by Graham Rosewarne

Artwork on page 2: Deinonychus

Photograph on page 29 by Sally A.Morgan; Ecoscene/CORBIS

Printed in the United States

Library of Congress Cataloging-in-Publication Data

Johnson, Jinny.
Velociraptor and other speedy killers / by Jinny Johnson.
p. cm. – (Dinosaurs alive!)
Includes index.
ISBN 978-1-59920-066-8
1. Velociraptor—Juvenile literature. I. Title.

QE862.S3J643 2007
567.912—dc22   2007007700

9 8 7 6 5 4 3 2

Contents

A dinosaur's world

A dinosaur was a kind of reptile that lived millions of years ago. Dinosaurs lived long before there were people on Earth.

We know about dinosaurs because many of their bones and teeth have been discovered. Scientists called paleontologists (pay-lee-on-tol-ojists) learn a lot about dinosaurs by studying these bones.

The first dinosaurs lived about 225 million years ago. They disappeared—became extinct—about 65 million years ago.

Some scientists believe that birds are a type of dinosaur, so they say there are still dinosaurs living all around us!

Ornithomimus

TRIASSIC
248 to 205 million years ago
Some dinosaurs that lived at this time:
Coelophysis, Eoraptor, Liliensternus,
Plateosaurus, Riojasaurus, Saltopus

EARLY JURASSIC
205 to 180 million years ago
Some dinosaurs that lived at this time:
Crylophosaurus, Dilophosaurus, Lesothosaurus,
Massospondylus, Scelidosaurus, Scutellosaurus

Lesothosaurus

LATE JURASSIC
180 to 144 million years ago
Some dinosaurs that lived at this time:
Allosaurus, Apatosaurus, Brachiosaurus,
Ornitholestes, Stegosaurus, Yangchuanosaurus

EARLY CRETACEOUS
144 to 98 million years ago
Some dinosaurs that lived at this time:
Baryonyx, Giganotosaurus, Iguanodon, Leaellynasaura,
Muttaburrasaurus, Nodosaurus, Sauropelta

LATE CRETACEOUS
98 to 65 million years ago
Some dinosaurs that lived at this time:
Ankylosaurus, Gallimimus, Maiasaura, Triceratops,
Tyrannosaurus, Velociraptor

Tyrannosaurus

5

Velociraptor

Not all meat-eating dinosaurs were giants.
The velociraptor was only about the size of a large
dog, but it was still a very fierce predator.

This dinosaur could run fast, standing
upright on its slender legs. It may have
hunted in packs.

The velociraptor is well-known today
because it had a starring role in the *Jurassic
Park* films. But the dinosaurs in the film were
much larger than the real-life velociraptor.

The dinosaur probably had a covering
of feathers, but it could not fly.

This is how you say
velociraptor:
vel-oss-ee-rap-tor

6

The velociraptor was a very agile dinosaur. It could leap on its prey and attack it with sharp claws.

VELOCIRAPTOR

Group: theropods (dromaeosaurs)

Length: up to 6 feet (1.8 m)

Lived in: Mongolia

When: Late Cretaceous, 84–80 million years ago

Inside a velociraptor

The velociraptor might have been small, but it was strong and a good hunter.

This predator had powerful jaws lined with about 80 teeth. The teeth had jagged edges for attacking prey and eating meat.

The velociraptor had three slender fingers with big claws on each hand.

Each foot had four toes, one with a large, curved claw twice the size of the others. The velociraptor held this claw off the ground when it was running so that it stayed sharp.

The velociraptor had many bones in its long tail to make it stronger. It held its tail straight out, like a rod, to help it balance as it ran.

The dinosaurs lived long before there were people on Earth. But here you can see how big the velociraptor was compared to a seven-year-old child.

A velociraptor in action

A pack of velociraptors hunting together could bring down animals much larger than themselves.

Experts once thought that the velociraptor slashed at the flesh of its prey with its claws. They now believe that the dinosaur killed by piercing the neck of its prey with a sharp claw.

Some fossils found in Mongolia showed a velociraptor battling with a protoceratops (pro-toe-serra-tops) dinosaur. The left claw of the velociraptor was plunged into the neck of the other dinosaur. The dinosaurs probably died together in a sandstorm that blew in as they were fighting.

Even fierce hunters, such as the velociraptor, didn't always win their battles. The protoceratops had a heavy, bony neck frill to protect it. It defended itself with its sharp beak.

Deinonychus and dromaeosaurus

These two dinosaurs were relatives of the velociraptor. They, too, were fast-moving hunters that could run on their strong back legs at 37 miles (60 km) an hour.

This is how you say dromaeosaurus: drom-ee-oh-sore-us

DROMAEOSAURUS

Group: theropods (dromaeosaurs)

Length: up to 6 feet (1.8 m)

Lived in: North America

When: Late Cretaceous, 76–74 million years ago

Both of these dinosaurs had light, strong bodies. They could jump on their prey or quickly move to dodge swinging tails or horns.

Fossilized skulls show that these dinosaurs had large brains for their size. They had good hearing, sharp eyes, and a strong sense of smell. These senses made them good hunters.

DEINONYCHUS

Group: theropods (dromaeosaurs)

Length: up to 10 feet (3 m)

Lived in: North America

When: Early Cretaceous, 120–110 million years ago

This is how you say deinonychus: die-non-eye-kus

Compsognathus

The speedy little compsognathus was one of the smallest dinosaurs. It was only about the size of a large chicken, but it had a long tail.

The compsognathus moved upright on its long, slender back legs. It could run and jump to escape from predators and capture prey. It was a good hunter and preyed on small creatures such as lizards.

The name compsognathus means "elegant jaw." The dinosaur's long jaws were lined with many small, sharp teeth. It also had clawed fingers on each hand.

This is how you say compsognathus: comp-sog-nath-us.

The remains of lizards have been found inside the stomachs of some compsognathus fossils.

COMPSOGNATHUS

Group: theropods (coelurosaurs)

Length: up to 26 inches (65 cm)

Lived in: Europe

When: Late Jurassic, 145–140 million years ago

Coelophysis

The coelophysis was one of the earliest meat-eating dinosaurs. Its name means "hollow form." It was given this name because its bones were partly hollow.

Hollow bones made the coelophysis very light, so it could run and jump as it hunted prey such as lizards, frogs, insects, and fish.

Sixty years ago, many coelophysis fossils were found together in New Mexico. Experts think that they probably hunted in packs, so they could attack larger animals.

Some of the fossils seemed to contain the bones of smaller coelophysis dinosaurs. But scientists think that the adults may have died with the young, perhaps during a flood or storm.

COELOPHYSIS

Group: theropods (coelurosaurs)

Length: up to 10 feet (3 m)

Lived in: North America

When: Late Triassic, 225–220 million years ago

This is how you say coelophysis:
see-low-fie-sis

The coelophysis raced around on its slender back legs, seizing prey with narrow-toothed jaws. It had short arms and three-fingered, clawed hands.

17

Gallimimus

The name gallimimus means "chicken mimic."
But the gallimimus was twice the size of an
ostrich, so it was much bigger than a chicken!

This lightly built dinosaur ran fast
on its slender back legs and was
an intelligent, sharp-eyed hunter.

The gallimimus had claws on its
hands and feet that it used to seize
prey such as lizards and insects.
It probably ate the eggs of other
dinosaurs as well as fruit and
leaves.

This is how you say
gallimimus:
ga-lee-mee-mus

The gallimimus did not have
teeth in its beak-like jaws, so it
swallowed its food whole.

GALLIMIMUS

Group: theropods
(ornithomimids)

Length: up to 20 feet (6 m)

Lived in: Asia

When: Late Cretaceous,
74–70 million years ago

The gallimimus was speedy enough to catch fast-moving prey such as lizards.

Struthiomimus and ornithomimus

Both of these dinosaurs were fast-moving hunters like the gallimimus. They did not have sharp teeth or massive claws, so they had to run fast to escape from predators.

STRUTHIOMIMUS

Group: theropods (ornithomimids)

Length: up to 13 feet (4 m)

Lived in: North America

When: Late Cretaceous, 76–74 million years ago

This is how you say struthiomimus: struth-ee-oh-mee-mus

These dinosaurs could probably run nearly 44 miles (71 km) an hour. That is much faster than the fastest human runners.

Both dinosaurs held their tails out behind them to balance the weight at the front of the body.

They had large eyes to help them spot danger as well as prey. They probably ate small creatures, such as lizards and insects, but they may have eaten leaves and fruits, too.

ORNITHOMIMUS

Group: theropods (ornithomimids)

Length: up to 13 feet (4 m)

Lived in: North America

When: Late Cretaceous, 76–74 million years ago

This is how you say ornithomimus:
orn-ith-oh-mee-mus

Oviraptor

The long-legged oviraptor was a fast dinosaur. It probably ate small animals, some plants, and eggs.

The oviraptor did not have teeth, but it did have very powerful jaws. Its jaws were shaped like a beak with sharp edges, so it could eat most types of food.

The oviraptor's name means "egg thief," but the dinosaur doesn't deserve this name.

The first fossils of oviraptors were found with a clutch of eggs, so it looked as though the oviraptor had been stealing the eggs from another dinosaur's nest. However, other fossils show that oviraptors did not steal eggs but protected their own.

OVIRAPTOR

Group: theropods (oviraptorids)

Length: up to 7 feet (2 m)

Lived in: Asia

When: Late Cretaceous, 85–75 million years ago

This is how you say oviraptor:
oh-vee-rap-tor

The oviraptor laid its eggs in a little hole in the ground and probably sat on the eggs to keep them warm and safe. The eggs had hard shells, just like a bird's egg.

Bambiraptor

A 14-year-old boy found the bones
of this dinosaur when he was
fossil hunting in Montana.

The dinosaur turned out to be a new
kind, and it was named bambiraptor
because of its small size.

*This little creature was an
agile hunter. It ran fast to
catch its prey, then held it
in clawed fingers and killed
it with one bite.*

BAMBIRAPTOR

Group: theropods (dromaeosaurs)

Length: up to 3 feet (1 m)

Lived in: North America

When: Late Cretaceous, 84–71 million years ago

This is how you say bambiraptor:
bam-be-rap-tor

The bambiraptor looked a lot like a bird. It had light, hollow bones and may have been covered with feathers.

The dinosaur ate lizards and small mammals. It had large claws on the second toe of each foot that helped it kill prey.

Caudipteryx

This bird-like dinosaur was about the size of a turkey, with long legs, short arms, and a short tail.

The caudipteryx was covered with feathers that could be eight inches (20 cm) long. It also had a fan of tail feathers. But the way the feathers were arranged on the body shows that the dinosaur could not fly.

This is how you say caudipteryx:
caw-dip-ter-iks

CAUDIPTERYX

Group: theropods (caudipterygid)

Length: up to 3 feet (1 m)

Lived in: China

When: Early Cretaceous, 125–122 million years ago

The caudipteryx had a small head with a beak and long, sharp teeth in its upper jaw.

The dinosaur may have swallowed stones to help grind up the food inside its body, much like crocodiles and some birds do today.

Some experts think the feathers kept the caudipteryx warm. Others believe that the dinosaur may have used its feathers to attract mates.

Dinosaurs and birds

Did you know that the birds you see flying around your yard are related to fierce meat-eating dinosaurs? That's what most scientists believe now.

Some experts have thought this for a long time, but their ideas were hard to prove. Then in 1997, fossils of some very special dinosaurs were found in China.

The fossils showed that these dinosaurs had feathers. They didn't have the proper wings for flying, but their feathery coats would have kept them warm and may have helped them attract mates.

The feathered dinosaurs, such as the caudipteryx, looked much like the deinonychus and other fast-moving, hunting dinosaurs. They proved that birds and some types of dinosaurs are very closely linked.

Experts now think that other meat-eating dinosaurs, such as the deinonychus and the struthiomimus, may have had feathers, too.

The feathered dinosaurs also looked a lot like the fossils of the first known bird—the archaeopteryx (ark-ee-op-ter-ix).

These fossils show a creature about the size of a blue jay. It had feathers like a bird and teeth and clawed fingers like a dinosaur. The fossils were found in Germany in 1861.

The archaeopteryx could fly, but may have had trouble taking off from the ground. It probably launched itself into the air from a tree. This picture shows one of the fossils found in Germany.

Words to know

Cretaceous
The period of time from 144 to 65 million years ago.

Fossils
Parts of an animal, such as bones and teeth, that have been preserved in rock for millions of years.

Horned dinosaur
A dinosaur with big, pointed horns on its head and a sheet of bone, called a frill, at the back of its head. The protoceratops was a horned dinosaur.

Jurassic
The period of time from 205 to 144 million years ago.

Neck frill
The sheet of bone at the back of a horned dinosaur's head.

Pack
Group of animals that ran around and hunted together.

Paleontologist
A scientist who looks for and studies fossils to find out more about the creatures of the past.

Predator
An animal that lives by hunting and killing
other animals.

Prey
Animals caught and killed by hunters such as the velociraptor.

Reptile
An animal with a backbone and a dry, scaly body.
Also, most reptiles lay eggs with leathery shells.
Dinosaurs were reptiles. Today's reptiles
include lizards, snakes, and crocodiles.

Scales
Covering on the body of a reptile. Scales are
made from keratin, like our fingernails.

Skull
The bony framework of an animal's head.

Triassic
The period of time from 248 to 205 million years
ago. The first dinosaurs lived in the Triassic period.

Index

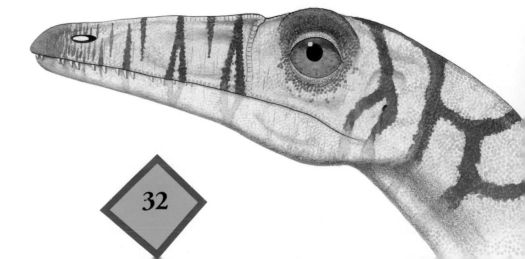